Oxford Read and Discover

Discover! **2**

In the Mountains

Richard Northcott

Contents

OXFORD
UNIVERSITY PRESS

OXFORD
UNIVERSITY PRESS

Great Clarendon Street, Oxford, OX2 6DP, United Kingdom

Oxford University Press is a department of the University of Oxford. It furthers the University's objective of excellence in research, scholarship, and education by publishing worldwide. Oxford is a registered trade mark of Oxford University Press in the UK and in certain other countries

ISBN: 978 0 19 464687 1

An Audio CD Pack containing this book and a CD is also available, ISBN: 978 0 19 464697 0

The CD has a choice of American and British English recordings of the complete text.

An accompanying Activity Book is also available, ISBN: 978 0 19 464677 2

Printed in China

This book is printed on paper from certified and well-managed sources

ACKNOWLEDGEMENTS

Illustrations by: Kelly Kennedy pp.4, 5, 14, 17; Alan Rowe pp.20, 22, 24, 26, 28, 30, 32, 34, 35, 38, 39.

The Publishers would also like to thank the following for their kind permission to reproduce photographs and other copyright material: Alamy pp.3 (hot mountain/© JORDI CAMÍ), 6 (Frans Lemmens); Corbis pp.5 (© Jim Sugar), 7 (stone house/© O. Alamany & E. Vicens), 11 (purple alpine flower/© Bernd Zoller/imagebroker), 16 (skiing/© Karl Weatherly), 17 (walking/© Jordan Siemens, sledding/© Pierre Jacques/Hemis), 18 (© François Pugnet/Kipa); FLPA p.9 (snow leopard/Jurgen & Christine Sihns); Getty Images pp.7 (rice terraces/Bertrand Rieger/hemis.fr), 12 (Robert McGouey/All Canada Photos), 13 (crevasse/Darryl Leniuk/The Image Bank), 14 (Cultura/Henn Photography), 15 (rafting/Douglas Pearson/The Image Bank), 19 (water/Gary Ombler/Dorling Kindersley); Naturepl.com pp.8, 9 (alpacas/Pete Oxford); Oxford University Press pp.3 (snowy mountain), 10 (conifers/needles), 13 (avalanche), 15 (mountain biker), 16 (snowboarding), 19 (bread/cheese/fruit/chocolate/hat/gloves/map/compass); Science Photo Library pp.4 (Alison Wright), 11 (yellow alpine flowers/Duncan Shaw).

 # Introduction

Some mountains are cold and snowy. Mountains can be hot and dry, too. Many big rivers come from the mountains. Mountains are amazing!

What animals live in the mountains? What can you do in the mountains? Are there mountains where you live?

 Now read and discover more about mountains!

 # Mountains

mountain

Earth's crust

Mountains are high places on Earth. Earth has a crust. Earth's crust moves very, very slowly. It can move up and make mountains.

Mountains are very high. Mount Everest is about 8,850 meters high. Mountains are very old, too. Some mountains are millions of years old.

Mount Everest

Volcanoes are mountains. A volcano is a hole in Earth's crust. Under Earth's crust there's hot rock. The hot rock comes out of the volcano. Volcanoes can be dangerous.

hot rock

Earth's crust

→ Go to pages 20–21 for activities.

 People

Living in the mountains can be difficult for people. High in the mountains, there aren't any big roads. Some people don't have a car. They use animals for transportation.

High in the mountains, some people don't have electricity.

Using Animals

A House

Look at this house. Now look at the mountains. They are the same color. People use rocks from the mountains to make their homes.

In the mountains, people grow food near their homes. Some people make terraces and they grow food there. On some terraces, there's lots of water. People grow rice in the water.

Rice on Terraces

→ Go to pages 22–23 for activities.

3 Animals

wing

A Golden Eagle

In the mountains you can see amazing animals. Golden eagles live in the mountains in Asia, North America, Africa, and Europe. They make nests on high rocks.

Golden eagles have big wings. They can fly very high. They can see very well, too. They eat small animals. From high in the sky, they can see small animals on the ground.

paw

A Snow Leopard

Many mountain animals have thick fur. Their fur helps them to stay warm.

Snow leopards live in the mountains in Asia. They have big paws with lots of fur. This fur helps them to walk on snow and ice.

Discover!

Alpacas live in the mountains in South America. Some alpacas have very thick fur!

Go to pages 24–25 for activities.

Plants

Conifers are a type of tree. Conifers don't have big leaves. They have small needles. On some snowy mountains, there are lots of conifers. Conifers can grow in cold places.

Very high in the mountains, it's very cold and windy. Trees can't live there.

Conifers

needles

Mountain Plants

Some plants can live very high in the mountains, but they are small. There isn't much rain, so the plants have long roots. The roots find water under the ground.

Some mountain plants make strong buds. The buds can stay under the snow in winter. After the winter, the buds come out of the snow. Then the buds open.

bud

→ Go to pages 26–27 for activities.

5 Ice and Snow

A Glacier

In the mountains you can see rivers of ice! A river of ice is called a glacier.

What makes a glacier? In winter, lots of snow falls on the mountains. Then, new snow falls on the old snow and makes ice. The ice moves down the mountain in a glacier. Glaciers move very, very slowly.

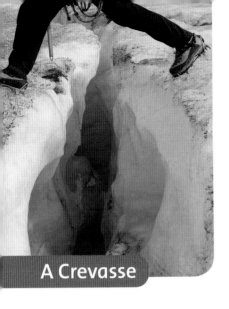

A Crevasse

In some glaciers, there are big crevasses. Crevasses are holes in the ice. Crevasses are dangerous. In snowy weather, people don't see a crevasse. Then they can fall in.

Avalanches are dangerous, too. In an avalanche, lots of snow falls from the mountain. It can fall on people.

An Avalanche

→ Go to pages 28–29 for activities.

 # Summer Sports

helmet

rope

A Climber

In summer, some people climb mountains. Climbers have a helmet and a rope.

Climbing is a difficult sport. Climbers have strong arms and legs. Climbers find good rocks for their hands and feet.

 Discover!

On some mountains there's snow in summer!

Mountain biking is a summer sport. Mountain bikes have big, strong wheels. The wheels are good on rocks.

Rafting is a great summer sport. For rafting, people have a helmet and a lifejacket. Rafts are very strong. They can go over rocks in the water.

Mountain Biking

wheel

Rafting

lifejacket

raft

→ Go to pages 30–31 for activities.

7 Winter Sports

Can you ski? Lots of children go skiing in the mountains in winter. They go with their family or with their school.

Snowboarding is a winter sport, too. Snowboarding is difficult. Snowboarders fall in the snow a lot. Good snowboarders can do amazing tricks.

Skiing

Snowboarding

snowshoe

Walking

sled

Sledding

Do you like walking in the mountains? You can walk in snowshoes. Snowshoes are big so you can walk on the snow.

Sledding is a great sport. You can go very fast on a sled.

 Discover!

In the Olympic Games, sleds can go at 140 kilometers an hour!

→ Go to pages 32–33 for activities.

8 Be Careful!

A Helicopter

Mountains can be dangerous. You can fall or get lost. In the mountains helicopters come and help people.

The weather in the mountains can be nice and sunny, but it can be cloudy and rainy, too. High in the mountains it is cold, so take warm clothes.

Take water when you walk in the mountains. Don't drink water from a river. Take food. It's good to eat cheese, bread, fruit, and chocolate. Take a map and a compass, too.

Have fun in the mountains, but be careful!

water

bread

fruit

cheese

chocolate

warm clothes

map

compass

→ Go to pages 34–35 for activities.

1 Mountains

← Read pages 4–5.

Earth   hole
million   ~~mountains~~
rock   volcano

1 Write the words.

1 _mountains_

2 _____

3 _____

4 _____

5 _____

6 _____

2 Circle the correct words.

1 Mountains are very high **meters** / (**places**) on Earth.

2 Earth's crust **moves** / **are** up and makes mountains.

3 Mount Everest is a very high **hole** / **mountain**.

4 Some mountains are **very** / **millions** of years old.

3 Complete the sentences.

dangerous   hole   ~~mountains~~   rock

1 Volcanoes are _mountains_ .

2 A volcano is a _____ in Earth's crust.

3 Hot _____ comes out of volcanoes.

4 Volcanoes can be _____ .

4 Order the words.

1 very / are / old. / Mountains
Mountains are very old.

2 high. / very / Mountains / are
_____

3 meters / 8,850 / is / high. / Mount Everest
_____

4 crust. / a / has / Earth
_____

5 slowly. / moves / crust / Earth's / very, / very
_____

6 Under / rock. / Earth's / hot / there's / crust
_____

② People

← Read pages 6–7.

1 **Write the words. Then match.**

1 c s r e e r a t

___terraces___

2 d o r a

_____

3 d o f o

_____

4 i t i c y t r e l e c

_____

2 **Find and write the words.**

mountaincaranimalhousewaterrice

1 ___mountain___   2 _____   3 _____

4 _____   5 _____   6 _____

3 Circle the correct words.

1 High in the mountains, there aren't any big rocks / (roads.)

2 Some people in the mountains use **terraces** / **animals** for transportation.

3 High in the mountains some people don't **have** / **grow** electricity.

4 People use **rocks** / **rice** for their houses.

5 People grow food **in** / **near** their homes.

6 Some people grow rice on **terraces** / **roads**.

4 Complete the sentences.

1 Some people in the mountains don't
   have a car.
   (car. / have / a)

2 Some people in the mountains _____
   _____
   (electricity. / don't / have)

3 People use rocks from the mountains to
   _____
   (homes. / their / make)

4 People make terraces _____
   (grow / and / food.)

3 Animals

← Read pages 8–9.

1 Complete the puzzle.

1 ↓

```
1     s
2 →   n       
      o
3 →           w
4 →           l
              e
              o
5 →           p
              a
6 →           r
              d
```

2 Write *true* or *false*.

1 Snow leopards can't walk on snow. _false_

2 Snow leopards have big paws. _____

3 Golden eagles don't make
  nests on high rocks. _____

4 Golden eagles can see very well. _____

5 Golden eagles fly high in the sky. _____

6 There aren't any alpacas
  in South America. _____

3 Complete the sentences.

> wings   walk   fur   South America

1 Snow leopards can _____ on snow and ice.
2 Golden eagles have big _____.
3 There are alpacas in_____.
4 Alpacas have very thick _____.

4 Answer the questions.

1 Where do snow leopards live?

They live in the mountains in Asia.

2 Where do golden eagles live?

_____

_____

3 Where do alpacas live?

_____

4 Are there snow leopards, golden eagles, or alpacas in your country?

_____

_____

④ Plants

← Read pages 10–11.

1 Write the words.

bud   leaves   needles
rain   roots   snow

1 _____

2 _____

3 _____

4 _____

5 _____

6 _____

2 Circle the correct words.

1 Conifers have small **needles** / **roots**.

2 Trees **can** / **can't** live very high in the mountains.

3 Some plants make strong buds. The buds come out of the **rain** / **snow**.

4 Roots find **needles** / **water** under the ground.

3 Match.

1 Conifers are
2 Conifers don't
3 Very high in the mountains,
4 Plants have long
5 There isn't much rain
6 Some mountain plants

high in the mountains.

make strong buds.

it's very cold and windy.

a type of tree.

have big leaves.

roots.

4 Order the words.

1 conifers / are / There / mountains. / in / the

_____

2 small / have / needles. / Conifers

_____

3 can / grow / Conifers / cold / places. / in

_____

4 mountains. / the / in / Some / plants / can / very / live / high

_____

⑤ Ice and Snow

← Read pages 12–13.

avalanche   fall
crevasse   glacier
river   slowly

1 Write the words.

1 _____

2 _____

3 _____

4 _____

5 _____

6 _____

2 Circle the correct words.

1 **Ice / Snow** falls in the mountains in winter.

2 New snow **falls / slowly** on old snow.

3 Ice **moves / makes** down the mountain in a glacier.

4 Glaciers move very, very **fast / slowly**.

3 Complete the sentences.

dangerous   ice   falls   weather

1 Crevasses are holes in the _____.

2 In snowy _____, people can fall in
  crevasses.

3 Avalanches are _____.

4 In an avalanche, lots of snow _____
  from the mountain.

4 Match. Then write the sentences.

A glacier is

Glaciers move

In some glaciers,

Crevasses are

very, very slowly.

dangerous.

a river of ice.

there are big
crevasses.

1 A glacier is a river of ice.

2 _____

3 _____

4 _____

6 Summer Sports

← Read pages 14–15.

1 **Write the words. Then match.**

1 e p o r

_____

2 h e w l e

_____

3 t r a f

_____

4 m e e l t h

_____

2 **Find and write the words.**

climberstrongbikegreatsportrocks

1 _____ 4 _____

2 _____ 5 _____

3 _____ 6 _____

3 Circle the correct words.

1 Climbers have a helmet and a **wheel** / **rope**.

2 Climbers have strong **arms** / **sports** and legs.

3 Mountain bikes **are** / **have** big, strong wheels.

4 Rafting is a great **winter** / **summer** sport.

5 On some mountains there's **snow** / **weather** in summer.

6 Climbers find good **rocks** / **wheels** for their hands and feet.

4 Complete the sentences.

1 Rafting is _____
   (great / a / summer / sport.)

2 Rafts _____
   (very / strong. / are)

3 Rafts can _____
   (over / rocks. / go)

4 Mountain bikes _____
   (wheels. / have / strong)

5 Do you _____
   (bike? / have / a / mountain)

7 Winter Sports

← Read pages 16–17.

1 Complete the puzzle.

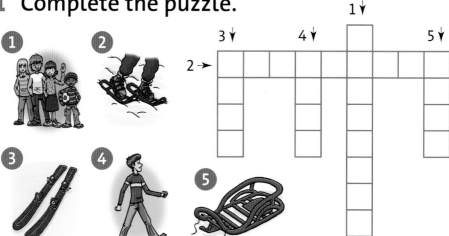

2 Write *true* or *false*.

1 Skiing isn't a winter sport. _____

2 Snowboarding is difficult. _____

3 Snowboarders can do
amazing tricks. _____

4 Snowshoes are big. _____

5 Snowshoes are big so you
can walk on the snow. _____

6 Sleds don't go very fast. _____

3 Complete the sentences.

> school   difficult   skiing   snow   walk

1 Some children go _____ in winter.

2 Some children go skiing with their _____.

3 Snowboarders fall in the _____ a lot.

4 Snowboarding is _____.

5 Some people _____ in snowshoes.

4 Order the words.

1 is / a / Sledding / sport. / great

_____

2 a / sled. / can / go / fast / You / on / very

_____

3 walking? / you / like / Do

_____

4 can / walk / You / in / snowshoes.

_____

5 snow. / fall / Snowboarders / the / in

_____

8 Be Careful!

← Read pages 18–19.

1 Write the words.

bread   cheese   compass
water   helicopter   map

1 _____

2 _____

3 _____

4 _____

5 _____

6 _____

2 Match.

1 You can get lost	the mountains.
2 Helicopters come	and help people.
3 Take food and water	when you walk in the mountains.
4 Don't drink water	from a river.
5 Be careful in	in the mountains.

3 Write the weather.

  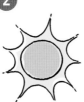

1 _It's snowy._   3 _____

2 _____   4 _____

4 What do you take when you walk in the mountains? Find and write the words.

w	a	t	e	r	e	b	r	e	a	d
g	c	h	o	c	o	l	a	t	e	h
r	t	c	f	r	u	i	t	h	k	z
d	e	c	h	e	e	s	e	n	t	f
n	r	v	r	q	s	m	a	p	r	j
w	a	r	m	c	l	o	t	h	e	s
c	o	m	p	a	s	s	m	k	w	t

1 _warm clothes_   5 _b_____

2 _c_____   6 _c_____

3 _w_____   7 _c_____

4 _f_____   8 _m_____

Project 1 An Animal Poster

1 Think of an animal in the mountains. Write the animal's name and draw a picture.

Name: _____

2 Answer the questions about the animal.

1 Where does it live? _____

2 Is it big or small? _____

3 What color is it? _____

4 Does it have fur? _____

5 What does it eat? _____

6 What can it do? _____

3 Make a poster about the animal.

4 Display your poster.

Project 2 A Mountain Fact File

1 Think of a mountain in your country.

2 Draw the mountain and write about it.

Name: _____

Animals	Plants
_____	_____
_____	_____
_____	_____

Sports	Weather
_____	_____
_____	_____
_____	_____

Picture Dictionary

climb

dangerous

down

dry

Earth

electricity

fall

fast

food

fur

ground

grow

high

hole

ice

leaves

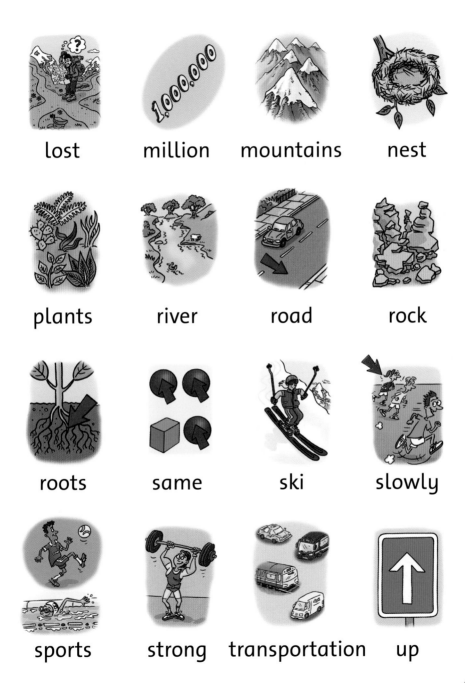

lost million mountains nest

plants river road rock

roots same ski slowly

sports strong transportation up

Oxford Read and Discover

Series Editor: Hazel Geatches • CLIL Adviser: John Clegg

Oxford Read and Discover graded readers are at six levels, for students from age 6 and older. They cover many topics within three subject areas, and support English across the curriculum, or Content and Language Integrated Learning (CLIL).

Available for each reader:
• Audio CD Pack (book & audio CD)
• Activity Book

Teaching notes & CLIL guidance: **www.oup.com/elt/teacher/readanddiscover**

Subject Area / Level	The World of Science & Technology	The Natural World	The World of Arts & Social Studies
① 300 headwords	• Eyes • Fruit • Trees • Wheels	• At the Beach • In the Sky • Wild Cats • Young Animals	• Art • Schools
② 450 headwords	• Electricity • Plastic • Sunny and Rainy • Your Body	• Camouflage • Earth • Farms • In the Mountains	• Cities • Jobs
③ 600 headwords	• How We Make Products • Sound and Music • Super Structures • Your Five Senses	• Amazing Minibeasts • Animals in the Air • Life in Rainforests • Wonderful Water	• Festivals Around the World • Free Time Around the World
④ 750 headwords	• All About Plants • How to Stay Healthy • Machines Then and Now • Why We Recycle	• All About Desert Life • All About Ocean Life • Animals at Night • Incredible Earth	• Animals in Art • Wonders of the Past
⑤ 900 headwords	• Materials to Products • Medicine Then and Now • Transportation Then and Now • Wild Weather	• All About Islands • Animal Life Cycles • Exploring Our World • Great Migrations	• Homes Around the World • Our World in Art
⑥ 1,050 headwords	• Cells and Microbes • Clothes Then and Now • Incredible Energy • Your Amazing Body	• All About Space • Caring for Our Planet • Earth Then and Now • Wonderful Ecosystems	• Food Around the World • Helping Around the World